Holy Spirit
my best
Friend

ATINUKE OMISADE

DEDICATION

THIS

BOOK IS DEDICATED TO

THE HOLY SPIRIT

WHO HAS BEEN TO ME

A COUNSELLOR, HELPER, TEACHER

AND MOST IMPORTANTLY,

MY BEST FRIEND.

CONTENTS

ACKNOWLEDGEMENTS

All the glory must go to God my heavenly father, and to Jesus, my Lord, King, Saviour and Healer. You brought me out of the miry clay and set my feet upon the rock.

My beloved husband and Pastor, Femi. You allowed me to answer the call to ministry and the freedom to be gloriously used in the service of my Master. Thank you.

I am grateful to my wonderful children. Antoinette, Anthony and John, for sharing me with other sons and daughters God has graciously brought to me. May you be a mighty host.

To my parents, Kayode & Roseline Adesola. (Dad's gone to be with the Lord). For inputting into me Christain values and raising me to love and fear the Lord.

To Rev. Dr. Paul and Rev. Mrs. Kate Jinadu, my wonderful parents in the Lord.

To Rev. & Rev. Mrs Timothy Kolade, for your continuous support and encouragement, and for releasing me into ministry.

To my church family, New Covenant Church, Old Kent Road, London.

To 'The Masters Touch' team, God bless you all.

To all those unnamed, who continuously encouraged me to write.

FOREWORD

As the author of the Bible, the Holy Spirit gives little insight into Himself, preferring rather to concentrate on the Father and the Son. Nevertheless, there is a lot under the surface that we can know about Him.

A head knowledge of the Holy Spirit cannot transform the heart, neither can it empower for ministry. Only a first hand encounter and daily walk with Him can bring that dynamism into our Christian experience.

Friendship with the Holy Spirit is not a luxury. It is of the utmost importance for the child of God. For Jesus said, "He will be with you forever." We need Him in heaven as much as we do here and now.

Jesus also said, "If any man thirst, let him come to me and drink." The missing link in knowing the Holy Spirit is this thirst. Without the thirst, which the Holy Spirit Himself creates in our hearts, our journey of discovery cannot begin.

It is books like this, written by someone with attested evidence of a balanced and consistent walk with the Holy Spirit that can aid us in our quest for that thirst.

Paul Jinadu

General Overseer, New Covenant Church.

"If you love me, you will obey what l command. And l will ask the Father, and he will give you another Counsellor to be with you forever – the Spirit of truth. The world cannot accept him, because it neither sees him nor knows him. But you know him, for he lives with you and will be in you. I will not leave you as orphans; I will come to you."

John 14:15-18 NIV

__INTRODUCTION__

I have always wanted to learn how to bake, especially cakes. I always stop to admire a well-iced cake and can't imagine anyone wanting to put a knife through such a beautiful display. The use of colours and the little decorative items made from sugar just seems to leave me in awe. In order not to get tempted, I keep well away from buying them except on special occasions of course, and besides, I'm always watching my weight.

Someone must have known my hearts desires because my dream came true one day in 1991, when through my mail an invitation came to learn not only to bake a cake, but also to ice it. It was to be a short weekend course. Even though my weekends were precious to me as I worked full time with two young children then, I could not resist the offer. I phoned in and was enrolled on the course and I thoroughly enjoyed myself. On the final day, we were asked to do a presentation. I baked a small 9" diameter sponge cake and iced it. We were asked to write whatever we wanted on the cake. Instead of the usual "Happy Birthday" etc, I wrote, "To HS my best friend." Everybody on the course wanted to know whom 'HS' is. There wasn't enough space on the cake to write the Holy Spirit, so I abbreviated it. When I told them what it meant, they thought I had lost my mind. You can't be serious one said. Another said, is that the name of a person? Some of them had never heard of the Holy Spirit up till this point, and those that knew simply could not understand how a "thing", a force or spirit, could be my best friend.

I kept the cake for weeks on end, not wanting to eat or throw it out. I have baked several cakes since then and found that they always turned out great. It has even been suggested that I go commercial by those who have tasted my cakes. There was a day I made a coconut cake with no effort whatsoever. I had not even had time to get out my scale to do any measuring of ingredients; I had simply slammed them all together in the bowl, mixed them up and baked. It turned out to be one of the best cakes I've ever baked. I began to ponder over why this was the case when the Holy Spirit whispered to my spirit these words, "Because you have honoured me by dedicating your first iced cake to me, I will honour you every time you bake a cake". I was amazed at that statement. It's only a cake, I thought to myself. How can it be that God in His Almightiness, creator of heaven and earth be interested in such a simple thing as an ordinary cake? But then, to the Holy Spirit, it was much more than that. It is recognising the fact that even in our day-to-day activities, the things we call mundane, the not so important things, the Holy Spirit still wants to be a part of them. It excites me to know he's interested in telling me where my lost keys or pen is. Saving me time searching endlessly for things I had misplaced and will probably never find had he not intervened.

He wants us to fellowship with him, to acknowledge his presence in our lives, to depend on him for all our needs, even in the baking of a cake.

How can it be that God in His Almightiness, creator of heaven and earth be interested in such a simple thing as an ordinary cake.

When I wrote those words on the cake, I meant them and still mean them today. He has remained my best friend, true and dependable.

Getting to this point in my life where I can refer to Him as my best friend did not happen overnight. It has been a journey, and I'm still discovering new things about Him everyday.

Who is your best friend? Can you refer to the Holy Spirit as a friend let alone your best friend?

There is so much to learn about the Holy Spirit. I am trusting that God will minister to you as I share what He has done in my life and who He is to me. If you're meeting Him for the first time, this book is aimed at introducing Him to you in the simplest way possible. I am in no way indicating that He is to be taken lightly, the Holy Spirit is God and should be reverenced as such. He wants to fellowship with you, love you and guide you in all your ways. He wants to be your friend.

I trust by His help you too will be able to say He is closer to you than a brother, you will discover the true meaning of friendship and you will find Him to be the lover of your soul.

<u>WHAT HAPPENED TO ME?</u>

I was born into a nominal Christian home, the third of six children. My parents were Anglicans, very religious and devoted to attending Church. As a child, I cannot remember missing Church any Sunday. In fact, we started our local church with three to four other families in the local area coming together and having church in a lounge. The children were immediately enrolled into the choir. There were only about five or six of us, but we were good and we had the best choirmaster. He was tough but knew his stuff. We had choir practice about twice a week and sang like angels every Sunday. The congregation began to grow until we were not able to fit in the lounge anymore, we eventually got a small hall and 'All Souls Church' was birthed in Bodija Estate, Ibadan, Nigeria.

At home our parents saw to it that we served the Lord. Looking back now, I shouldn't have expected anything less. My dad was a choirboy when he was growing up. He knew everything about church and loved the Lord. My mum was born into a family of reverends and pastors. Her great-grandfather Rev. Daniel Olubi, working with missionaries Rev. David Hinderer and others brought Christianity to Abeokuta Nigeria in 1851. Her grandfather and father were both ordained men of God. So you see, we had no choice but to be in Church. She was bringing us up the only way she knew. Prayer bells rang every morning at six a.m. and we had to be there. For about an hour, we sang praise songs, read the psalms, prayed and listened to a sermon either by my dad or mum. We all hated it. How do you expect a six year old to be up as early as six am, on their feet, supposedly praising God? We couldn't understand why God would make such a demand on us when other children in other households were still having their beauty sleep. To make matters worse, Sunday didn't start on Sunday. It started on Saturday when we needed to iron our clothes for church and get our shoes polished and our hats sorted out. I detested those hats and I guess I've worn enough of them as a child to last a lifetime.

> *Sunday didn't start on Sunday, it started on Saturday when we needed to iron our clothes for church, and get our shoes polished.*

We had to be on our best behaviour in church, our parents were church leaders and we were little choristers. I loved singing, enjoyed dressing up for church on Sunday and looked forward to the special Sunday lunch, usually rice and chicken. I always felt there was more to church than dressing up every Sunday just to go and perform. It had become a performance and we loved to be applauded. I thought I knew God and my service in church was enough to buy me salvation. But all that changed one day. It was a Friday afternoon, Good Friday 1968 to be specific. I was watching the film 'Jesus of Nazareth' on our local TV channel as we did every Easter. My parents made us fast every Good Friday till 3.00pm in honour of the death of our Lord Jesus Christ. The film usually came on just after noon to end at about 3.00pm, which is the time Jesus died. It must have been the only film the Television Broadcasting Corporation had as they repeated it every year. Mum allowed us to watch the whole length of the film (about 3 hours) as long as we completed our chores before 12 noon.

The Good Friday chores included grating coconut, which is to be used in a beans based meal called 'Fridjon', and helping in making the special fish stew with which fridjon is served. We were not allowed to eat meat on this day.

As children, we could not really sit for three continuous hours watching the film, so we would usually go in and out of the lounge to do other things. We didn't seem to miss anything because as I said, we had watched it many times and knew what would happen next. This time around though, for reasons I can't explain, I was 'hooked' on the film. I was not only hooked, I was involved. I was in the film, a part of the crowd. I saw Jesus suffer for an offence he didn't commit, I saw him carry that heavy cross and saw him nailed on it. I heard myself with tears in my eyes say I was sorry He had to die. I wept and wept watching the film. It all so real. I was not aware of anyone else in the room with me. I had just had an experience I could not explain. I had met the Lord Jesus Christ and I didn't even know it.

We all grew up and began to leave home one by one. I had completed my secondary school education in 1975 and wanted to go to the United Kingdom to further my education. I always wanted to be an Architect and will therefore need to study for a two year General certificate of Education Advanced Level Course (commonly referred to as 'A' levels), before I can gain admission into university in the UK. However, you could get into University in Nigeria also by undergoing a one-year 'preliminary' course and I had gained admission into University of Ife, Nigeria to study Social Sciences. My parents felt it was a better option for me to remain in Nigeria. I was not happy with their decision because this would mean I could no longer study architecture, but I had to agree with them, as I would need their financial support if I was to go abroad.

I went ahead and started my first year in University. I attended church on campus every Sunday and prayed every day as I had been taught. In May 1976, a friend invited me to a fellowship on campus led by one of the lecturers. She promised the whole service would take about an hour. This sounded good to me, as the Sunday service in my Church will normally take up to two or more hours. For a student with examinations just round the corner, this was too much time to give, so I agreed to go with her. I enjoyed the teaching. All the man who led the meeting talked about was Jesus and how we needed a personal relationship with him. I thought I had this relationship already because I was a 'good' person, attend church regularly and I truly believed I was a Christian in the true sense of the word. He made a call for anyone who wanted to 'give their life to Jesus' to come forward. I'm really not sure why I felt the need to go forward that day, but I did anyway. I went forward with a few others and we were all led in a prayer of repentance of sin. We were asked to accept Jesus into our lives as Lord and Saviour, and the man then prayed for us, receiving us into the Kingdom of God. He said we were now 'born again' and then offered to pray with us for the baptism of the Holy Spirit, explaining that we would speak a heavenly language known as 'tongues'. I was not sure of what he meant by this, so I declined the offer. I have heard people of some religious sect speak what I regarded as gibberish in the past, shaking and looking totally out of control.

I thought he might be talking about the same thing. Apart from that, I hadn't quite figured out what being born again meant.

___

Who is the Holy Spirit, and why would I want to speak in some strange language?

___

He prayed with those that consented, and they began to speak this 'heavenly language'. I noticed they did not behave as I had expected, but seemed to be full of joy and some sort of peace. Everyone in the room rejoiced as if something really spectacular had happened! Who is the Holy Spirit and why would I want to speak in some strange language? I asked myself.

I left the meeting determined not to return. I wish now that somebody from the fellowship had spent some time explaining what happened to me and how to go on from there. I did not know that I was now a new creation and the Holy Spirit had come to dwell in me. I never went back, but I knew one thing, something had happened to me and I could not explain it.

WHAT ARE THESE 'GOOSE PIMPLES'?

✧

'What is wrong with me? Why am I so happy? Why can't I stop singing?' I kept asking myself these questions, looking for answers to the reason my life changed overnight. I was not an unhappy person, but now I was singing hymns in the shower. Sure enough everyone knew I was a Christian but not a fanatic. I was able to associate the change in my life with my visit to the fellowship, but I didn't want to go back to them because I was scared. Had I joined a cult? Who can I talk to? Who can explain all these to me? It suddenly occurred to me to talk to God. Of course, he hears us when we pray we've been told many times. So I got on my knees and prayed something like this ' Heavenly Father, I don't understand what is going on in my life these past few days' and suddenly, I felt like I had goose pimples all over me. What is going on? This is not the first time I've prayed. I've never been covered with goose pimples. Every time I tried to pray after then, the goose pimples would come. I resigned myself to the fact that I might have to live with this new experience all my life.

First year in University ended and I was still talking to my parents about Architecture. They came to realise that I was not going to let it go, so they agreed to send me abroad. Summer 1976, I was in London, England, waiting to start my 'A' levels in September.

I attended Ellerslie School in Malvern, Worcestershire. I immediately joined the school choir and Christian fellowship that met once a week led by the school chaplain. As soon as we started singing and praising God, I started feeling 'high', and the goose pimples came back. 'What are these goose pimples I asked myself?' I thought I had left them in Nigeria but they seem to have followed me over to England. 'The school chaplain will know, 'I told myself'. He's a man of God and should under-stand spiritual things'. So after fellowship one week, I told him what I had been experiencing and to my total disappointment, he told me he could not explain it. He however referred me to the school nurse, as he believed it was due to a change of climate. I was prescribed 'paracetamol', a painkiller.

That was the last straw; I was making an utter fool of myself. What will the chaplain think about me now, he might even tell the other girls, and they may all think I'm nuts or perhaps possessed.

I stopped going to fellowship and nobody bothered to find out why. I decided on just reading my bible every night, no prayers, no singing and that should be sufficient. Then I realised reading my bible had the same effect, it was as if someone was trying to speak to me, to draw my attention to something or someone I didn't know. This was more than I could handle, I packed up my bible, and that was it for the next ten years.

Life went on as usual, I went to Canterbury School of Architecture and studied architecture, did what students do, experimented with alcohol, partied all night, lived carelessly and the last thing on my mind was God. I still believed in God but didn't know how to reach Him. I truly believe He is always watching over us whether we know it or not. The fact that I had accepted Jesus into my life in 1976 qualified me to call on Him and be assured that He would be there for me, but I didn't know that at the time. However, an experience I had in 1981 fully convinces me that there is power in the name of Jesus. It was about 8:40 in the morning and I was dressed ready to attend lectures. My friend and classmate who lived in the flat above mine will normally knock on my door at about 10 minutes to 9. It was only a five-minute walk from the flat to our lecture rooms. Since I had about 10 minutes to wait, I laid down on my bed listening to some music. I could see the side road that leads to my flat from my window, however it was not possible to come right up to my window from the road because there was a flat in the basement which got its natural light from that side of the road. As I laid there starring out the window, I saw seven people walk into the road and I counted them one after the other as they were all in a row. They were all of African descent and there were only few blacks in Canterbury at that time, and so I was quite intrigued to see so many at the same time. I attempted to get off my bed to see if I could assist them in any way when I realised I could not move my body and besides, they had all filed in through my window, which as I said, was physically impossible. They just basically walked through the wall. At this point, I could no longer physically see them, but I knew I was not alone in the room. The next thing I knew was that I was being lifted off my bed, not as in being carried, but that my spirit was leaving my body. I was aware of the fact that my body was still on the bed, but at the same time, I knew I was "floating". I also knew I was dying and would have to do something to stay alive, however I was not in control of the activities going on around me. Just then, like a flash, I remembered the name of Jesus, and I heard myself shout JESUS. Suddenly, I slumped back unto my bed as if I was thrown from a distance and I was able to move my body again. It all happened very quickly because when I checked my clock, it was about 5 minutes past 9. My friend should have been at my door at 10 to 9. I wondered why she didn't come because if she had pressed my doorbell, perhaps all this will not have happened. I was ruffled and began to panic and then looking out of my window, I saw her coming towards the flat with another classmate. I rushed to the door to let them in and she said she had been to the flat at 10 minutes to 9 and my doorbell did not ring. She knocked on the door a couple of times and decided I had gone ahead of her, however when she got to the lecture hall and didn't see me, she was concerned and decided to ask one of the boys to come back with her. We went on to check the doorbell, which rang instantly. I recounted what had happened to me and they said I must have had a bad dream even though they could not explain the issue of the doorbell. It was not a dream, I was not even sleeping, it was a clear vision and I know the name of Jesus had set me free.

Spiritual things are real. A lot of people go to bed well and hearty, but are found dead in the morning.

Spiritual things are real. A lot of people go to bed well and hearty, but are found dead in their beds in the morning. I don't doubt that some of them probably had similar experiences. I may not be able to explain all that happened to me that day, but I thank God for sparing my life. This has certainly been one of the most incredible experiences I have ever had. The bible says in Philippians 2: 9-10:

'Therefore God has highly exalted Him and given Him the name which is above every name, that at the name of Jesus every knee should bow, of those in heaven, and of those on earth, and of those under the earth.'

It's the name above every name, the name at which every knee bows. The name of the Lord is a strong tower, the righteous run into His name and they are saved. I was shaken from the experience, but after a few weeks, I settled down into my usual routine and focused on my studies.

I met my husband Femi, also an architect in 1981. I graduated in 1984, and we were married in 1985. We decided to make our home in Nigeria. We had our first child; a beautiful baby girl, Antoinette Olufunke and everything seemed to be going on just fine until I became pregnant with my second child in 1987. I was so ill and in bed for most of the time.

About the 4th/5th month of the pregnancy, my brother came to see me full of excitement and joy. He said he had just given his life to Jesus; 'saved' as he put it, and it was so wonderful he couldn't keep it to himself. He began to share the good news with me, and almost immediately, I remembered 1976, my visit to the fellowship, the joy I had and the goose pimples. The same thing had happened to me then I thought. He said if I said a prayer after him, I too would be saved. I explained to him that I had been led in prayer in 1976 but didn't understand what had happened to me. However, I was willing to go over the whole process again. I was too ill to say no to anything at this point. As we began to pray together, I burst out in that language I had run away from those many years ago. I was speaking in 'tongues'. Even though I still didn't understand what was going on, this time around, I had a real peace about the whole thing. It wasn't just me, my brother had experienced the same thing, and somehow, that makes it seem all right.

God saw me through the pregnancy and in November 1987, we had our second child, Anthony Ayodeji.

It took another year before I was able to truly begin to seek God and find out what his plans for my life was. There was so much to learn. Jesus turned out to be so real. The bible actually began to make sense to me. There were men and women who had been born again for some time in the Full Gospel Businessmen's Fellowship, and they were teaching us so much about being a Christian. I discovered I was never really a Christian. Going to church regularly does not make you a Christian. I was a church - goer but had no relationship with Jesus. I was determined to make it up to the Lord for all those years I had wasted doing my own thing.

<u>WHO IS THE HOLY SPIRIT?</u>

The children and I relocated to the United Kingdom in 1989. We started attending Kensington Temple, an Elim Pentecostal church in London. I began to grow in the Word. I attended Sunday services and bible study religiously, read and studied the bible and many books that could benefit me, and attended various retreats. I was hungry for more of the Lord.

I knew Jesus was the Son of God and had died for me and paid the penalty for my sins. I found it comfortable praying to God and related to Him on a father to daughter basis. I had no problem loving Him and receiving His love because I had a great relationship with my natural dad. He went to be with the Lord in April 2000 and heaven must have rejoiced to have him home. He was the best dad on earth and did all he could to bring joy and laughter into the home all the time. I even remember him taking us to football matches at weekends so we could be with him.

Because he worked away from home and came home only at weekends, he always tried to make the most of the time we spent together. I was never afraid of my dad and knew that he cared for and loved me. He taught me to depend on God for all things and demonstrated his love for God by the many ways he blessed the church during his lifetime. Daddy knew most of the Psalms by heart, loved to sing and stayed up most nights praying. He was very compassionate and helped a lot of people achieve their goals in life. This helped me in my relationship with my heavenly father.

What does it mean to pray by the Holy Spirit?

It was easy for me to pray to God and Jesus, and I was quite happy doing so until I heard someone make a statement one day about praying to God through Jesus by the Holy Spirit. 'By the Holy Spirit'? What does it mean to pray by the Holy Spirit? How does He fit into the picture? I know according to scriptures three distinct Persons emerge, each of whom is God. God the Father, God the Son and God the Holy Spirit. I also know that He was introduced to us in the book of Genesis chapter 1, "And the Spirit of God was hovering over the face of the waters". (Gen.1: 2). Yes I've heard about the Trinity, but who is the Holy Spirit? The more I wanted to find out, the more confused I got. Nobody seemed to know much about Him, at least not anybody I know. Was I meant to pray to Him as well? Is this what is meant by fellowshipping with the Holy Spirit?

Is this what the 'goose pimples' is about? Will it all come back?

I was so desperate to find out more I visited the church bookshop after service the next Sunday. I went to the section on the Holy Spirit and one book stood out among the others, 'Good Morning Holy Spirit' by Benny Hinn. I've never heard of Pastor Benny Hinn at this point, but that book had something about it I couldn't explain. I bought it and started reading it that same day. By the next day, I had read the whole book. In summary, Benny explained how he met the Holy Spirit, he described the strange sensation he had in his bedroom and it reminded me of the goose pimples experience. He said He, the Holy Spirit is a person and he actually says 'Good morning' to him every morning. He explained that he wanted to fellowship with me and would explain the bible to me. I read that he is the power of God, a gentleman who will only come if invited. He also said He will reveal Jesus to me, speak to me through my spirit and guide me in the way I should go. There was so much to take in, but for the first time, I found somebody, a book, so simple yet so powerful that could explain to me what was missing in my life.

I wanted to meet Him so badly I put the children to bed earlier than usual that day and shut myself up in my room. If Benny had met him in his bedroom, there was no better place for me to arrange a meeting than my bedroom. Of course I didn't know at that time the Holy Spirit was everywhere let alone that He dwelt inside of me.

It was a cold winter night, so I tucked in under my duvet. I said, Holy Spirit, Benny Hinn says you are a person and if I invite you to come, you will, please show me he's right and that you're really there and want to fellowship with me'. It wasn't a prayer, they were just simple words but I meant every word.

I actually expected something to happen but I didn't know what or how or when. But to me it seemed almost instantly, I felt a warm embrace all over me. It was as if somebody had put his or her arms around me and I felt I had been wrapped in a warm electric blanket. Was I imagining things or was He truly honouring my invitation? At first I was a little afraid, not wanting to open my eyes just in case. Just in case what? In case Jesus was standing right there in my room. But there was a kind of peace, a knowing in my spirit it was OK not to be afraid, so I wasn't. I knew the Lord had put His loving arms around me and I felt His love. I didn't say anything, I couldn't, even if I wanted to, but then I didn't need to. I just knew everything about my life was going to be fine from now on, and I fell asleep in this state.

---

*There and then, I knew my life had
changed forever, and my destiny had been
altered.*

I woke up the next morning and repeated
Benny's words in welcoming the Holy Spirit. 'Good
Morning Holy Spirit' I said. There and then, I knew
my life had changed forever and my destiny had
been altered. I recognised the fact that I had a friend
I could talk to and who understood me clearly. He
was real, a Person. I couldn't see Him but I knew
He was present. I then made a conscious decision to
relate to Him as I would if I could see Him. I finally
understood the goose pimples, it was the Holy Spirit
trying to make himself known to me, He wanted my

fellowship with Him, to teach me the things I did not know, to reveal Jesus to me.

I began from that point on to study more. I discovered there were many books that taught on the Holy Spirit and there were deeper things I needed to learn and know. I am grateful to God for the book "Good Morning Holy Spirit". God had me in mind when Pastor Benny put that book together, he wrote it just for me.

My journey into finding out more about the Holy Spirit began from this point on.

GETTING TO KNOW HIM

Between 1989 and 1991, I was in training. It was a time of preparation, getting grounded in the Word. Joshua 1:8 says,

> 'This book of the Law shall not depart from your mouth, but you shall meditate in it day and night, that you may observe to do according to all that is written in it. For then you will make your way prosperous, and then you will have good success'.

My sister and I started a house group and this gave me the opportunity of sharing my experiences with other people. We met every Sunday evening in her lounge. The fellowship began to grow until we could no longer fit in the lounge. We went ahead and hired a church hall and before long, there were enough people to start a church. The fellowship helped me practise what I had learnt so to speak. God was always faithful. I began to see the gift of the spirit operate in me.

I remember the first time I prophesied, I was so humbled by the experience that I left the fellowship immediately after the meeting. I did not want anybody to say anything to me. In fact, I was so afraid and thought I had said the wrong words. What if I got it all wrong? Was I sure that was God speaking through me. 'Why did He have to pick on me on this particular day, after all, there were more mature Christians there He could have used?' So many thoughts flashed through my mind as I hurried home that evening. Not long after I got home, two of the brothers from the fellowship were at my door. I knew it, I said to myself, they've come to warn me or ban me from ever prophesying again. They seemed quite happy as they sat down and explained to me what had happened to me. Prophesying is to be greatly desired they said quoting 1Corinthians 14:1,

'Pursue love, and desire spiritual gifts, but especially that you may prophesy'.

The following Sunday, they gave me a book on spiritual gifts, which helped me understand further what the Holy Spirit Himself and some men and women of God had taught me. The more of the gifts of the spirit you exercise, the more God reveals to you and the more you are trusted with greater responsibilities.

All of a sudden, without anybody touching
Or going near them, the doors flung open,
A gush of wind rushed in, and the glory
Of God filled the room.

The first experience I had of God imparting me with a spiritual gift for service was at a fellowship meeting we had late 1990. Dr. Friday Nwator, a medical doctor turned preacher, who had devoted his life to serving God, had been teaching on the Holy Spirit. I was an usher at the event and had been manning the door, so I was right at the back.

All of a sudden, without anybody touching or going near them, the doors flung open and a gush of wind rushed in, and the power of God just filled the room. Some people burst out in tongues, others were on their faces praising God and I just lifted my hands up in worship. This was the way the Holy Spirit was poured out in the book of Acts 2:

> "When the day of Pentecost had fully come, they were all in one accord in one place. And suddenly there came a sound from heaven, as of a rushing mighty wind, and it filled the whole house where they were sitting."

I had never seen anything like this in my life. I noticed that my hands began to feel a sensation. A few minutes later, I could not move them at all, they were as heavy as lead. I approached the minister after the meeting and explained what had happened to me. He simply said, "God is anointing your hands to heal the sick, you will operate in the healing ministry". All that was happening to me at the time was more than I could understand. I was just coming to terms with prophesying and studying the gifts of the spirit, now he was talking about the healing ministry.

The bible says in 1 Corinthians 12:11, talking about spiritual gifts,

"But one and the same Spirit works in all these things, distributing to each one individually as He wills."

It is the Holy Spirit who determines what gift we get. It is as he wills.

I can understand God wanting to bless me with this gift. I am humbled that He is able to commit such an awesome ministry into my hands. I have been through pain, sickness and diseases myself. If the enemy had his way, I would have been terminated at pregnancy. My mum was nursing my sister who was 3 months old when she got pregnant with me. She didn't know she was pregnant but didn't feel well, so she went back to the hospital and they carried out a 'D&C' (Dilatation and Curettage) on her. They later found out it was a pregnancy and that I had survived. God had plans for my life.

"Before I formed you in the womb I knew you". Jeremiah 1:5

I can't remember having much fun as a child. I was always kept indoors because I was allergic to dust, pollen, grass and whatever else I came across. I watched other children run around, but if I tried to join in, the pain I would suffer afterwards persuaded me to keep away. I had sinuses so I was never without tissue to blow my nose. Fear also crept into my life, the fear of running out of tissue to blow my nose. How ridiculous you may say, but it's the truth. Nobody can understand how distressing it is to spend the whole day sneezing. I cannot remember a single day I did not sneeze. It was not only painful it was also embarrassing. As if those were not enough, I also had asthma, chest pains and backache.

I had sinuses, asthma, chest pains, back-ache – basically, what is referred to as 'the spirit of infirmity'.

These ailments continued into secondary school (I went to a boarding school), and every now and again, I would come up with a high fever and be sent home from school. My parents and the doctors did all they could, but basically, I had what the bible refers to as the 'spirit of infirmity'. Those were difficult times and I remember telling the Lord on one occasion that if I could not live a normal life, he should let me die. He chose to let me live. After all, He's the giver of life. The enemy comes to kill, steal and destroy, but Jesus came that I might have life and have it in abundance. I cannot tell you the exact day I received my healing, but I was set free from all those terrible pains one after the other. Every single one of them had left my body. I believe in divine healing, and I stay in divine health now. If you are sick in your body, trust God for your healing. As you walk with the Holy Spirit, you too will be set free. God is no respecter of persons. This is why I have such a passion to see sick people healed. I've been through it and I know it's not the best state to be. Besides, I know it is God's will for His children to be well.

I had come to love and trust the Holy Spirit. It's a two-way relationship. I play my role and He plays his. I continued to study the bible and began to listen to His spirit within me and obey instructions. The Old Testament seemed quite confusing at the time so I asked a lot of questions. I found that as I asked,

I got the answers from my heart; it will be just like having a thought about something. I began to understand how to listen to the voice of God. He communicates with us through our spirit because He dwells in our spirit.

> "But you are not in the flesh but in the Spirit, if indeed the Spirit of God dwells in you. Now if anyone does not have the Spirit of Christ, he is not His." Romans 8:9

When we become born again, the Spirit of God mingles or is united with our spirit. We now have access to the still small voice of God. We have a knowing about certain things, and that is why we often say 'something' told me to do this or not to do this. Obedience to the voice of the Spirit now plays a major role in our lives. Most times we hear God but don't obey because we haven't learnt to trust His voice, we're not sure whose voice we hear. I found the easiest way to learn is to be obedient anyway. I didn't always get it right, but a lot of time I did. That far outweighs my wishing I had been obedient.

Man is made up of spirit, soul and body and there is a difference between them.

"Now may the God of peace Himself sanctify you completely; and may your whole spirit, soul and body be preserved blameless at the coming of our Lord Jesus Christ." 1 Thessalonians 5:23

We are spirit; we have a soul and live in a body. The Holy Spirit unites with our spirit and 'govern' the soul so to speak. Before we became Christians, our soul wants to rule and be in control. To hear God, our souls must submit to the spirit. It must be quiet. We need to begin to train our spirit to be strong. I found that as I meditated on the Word of God, practised what I studied, gave the Word first place in my life and instantly obeyed the voice of the spirit, I began to mature spiritually. It is important that you learn to obey your spirit. Remember, learning takes time.

In announcing the coming of the Holy Spirit, Jesus referred to him in John 14:16 as the "Comforter". Isn't it refreshing to know that there is one who can and will bring comfort to our hearts when we are troubled. He will not simply sympathise but also heal us wherever we need healing. He doesn't only bring comfort, but is our companion, one who strengthens and walks alongside us.

I learnt a lot from the Holy Spirit Himself. Reading from the gospel of John 14:15-17 Jesus said,

"If you love me, keep my commandments. And I will pray the Father And he will give you another Helper, that He may abide with you Forever- the Spirit of truth, whom the world cannot receive, because It neither sees Him nor knows him, but you know him for he dwells with you And will be in you. I will not leave you orphans; I will come to you".

Jesus promised He would send us a Divine Helper/ Counsellor, 'the Spirit of truth'. The word helper means to aid, assist, encourage, support. He wants to guide and advise us in everything we do. He has proved to be everything Jesus said He is. He has often prompted me when I've left things undone. Several times he's alerted me when I've mistakenly left the key in the front door, left the cooker on and when there's danger ahead. On every occasion, He's been just as Jesus said He is. These experiences have helped me to identify and trust His voice. You may ask, but how does He speak? In those situations, it was through my spirit. It comes as a thought to me and I simply obey and check out what I hear.

I remember a particular winter morning. It had snowed lightly and the roads were quite slippery. I had taken the children to school and was returning back home. I took my usual route but kept getting a nudge in my spirit to go through the park. That meant a longer walk and so I immediately ignored my spirit. The nudging got stronger and I decided to be obedient. I turned back and headed for the route through the park. A few minutes later, there was a big crash on the park fence, a big white van had lost control and crashed into the fence. It suddenly dawned on me that had I continued walking down my regular route, I would have been hit by that van. I was greatly humbled and knew once more how much God loves me and want to protect me. However, I learnt that for Him to protect me, I had to be obedient to His voice.

"Your ears shall hear a word behind you saying, this is the way; walk in it"

Isaiah 30:21

Whether He speaks to you through the scriptures, through a friend, your pastor, a dream or through your life circumstances, He's always communicating with the heart that seeks Him. In every decision I've had to make, I've relied on the help of the Holy Spirit. Jesus said He's my Helper, so I've simply allowed Him to lead me since He knows all things. People say to me how did you know this or that, and I say the Holy Spirit revealed it to me. He is the Spirit of revelation. God wants us to know His plans and purposes for our lives. He said, 'I will not leave you as orphans'.

Knowing God is different from knowing about Him.

To know His plans for you, you need to know Him. Knowing God is different from knowing about

Him. Knowing Him means you have an intimate relationship with Him. It means He's the first person you think of in the morning as you wake up, and the last person before you go to bed. You listen for His instructions throughout the day and believe me, He wants to lead you, guide you and show you the way.

I don't always get it right. Just like anybody else, I sometimes miss His instructions too. However, in order to stay on course and be pleasing to God, I make sure I repent when I've missed Him. God is interested in every little detail. There are certain things that I got away with last year that I cannot do and get away with this year. If we are to be a light to the world, then we need to live by example.

I went shopping one day in our local supermarket. I had picked up some tinned peas but when I got to the frozen food section, I changed my mind and decided to go for frozen ones. Without thinking, I removed the tinned peas from my trolley, stacked them up in the open shelf next to the freezers and loaded my trolley with frozen peas. As I turned to carry on with my shopping, the Holy Spirit said to me, don't you think it will be nicer if you put back the tins in the compartment you took them from? I argued that it will take too long for me to walk all the way back to aisle number one when I was now in thirty, and besides, that should be the job of the shop assistants who looked to me like they weren't busy anyway. He said to me it isn't my business judging the shop assistants at this time, my business is to represent Christ and I wasn't doing a good job of that right now. I further argued that I was in a hurry anyway and couldn't possibly go back. There was total silence after that. The Holy Spirit is a gentleman. He will not force you to do anything you don't want to do. I tried to carry on with my shopping but couldn't. I had lost my peace and I knew until I obeyed, I wouldn't feel fine. I eventually obeyed. He's the Spirit of conviction and convicts us when we miss it.

God has used my local supermarket to teach me to walk right with Him. I have since been convicted of several other things including wanting to park in an area for disabled drivers, and not returning my trolley to the right place.

The Holy Spirit is a gentleman.
He will not force you to do anything you
don't want to do.

The Holy Spirit is truth, He wants to reveal the truth to us. The things we need to know and those we need to do away with. Remember, Satan is the liar, the bible says he's 'a liar and the father of it'. Jesus says the world cannot receive Him for they don't know Him. No wonder most people think we've lost it when we try to explain the Holy Spirit, they simply cannot understand us. But Jesus said we know Him, for he dwells with us and lives in us.

As a Christian, we should know the Holy Spirit and have fellowship with him. As we communicate with him, we will get to know Him better and He'll bear witness to our spirit about many things.

__GOING DEEPER__

It's been sixteen years now since I felt the warm embrace of the Holy Spirit in my bedroom. Everyday has been a new experience since then. I fell in love with Him, and I have not regretted a single moment of laying my life down for His service.

God has done some tremendous things in my life in all these years. He ordered my steps accordingly and showed me the way to go. The Holy Spirit has indeed proved to be my Guide and Helper. He granted me my hearts desires, one of which is to see my husband come to the Lord.

Femi had been brought up a Catholic and attended our local SS Peter and Paul Church. We had both received many invitations to attend the Full Gospel Businessmen's Fellowship International meetings and we had turned down every invite. However, when I re-dedicated my life to the Lord in 1987, I started attending the meetings until I relocated in 1989. In 1990, he accepted to attend a Full Gospel Businessmen's Fellowship International (FGBMFI) meeting where a man of God, Rev. Dr. Paul Jinadu, the General Overseer of the New Covenant Church ministered and he surrendered his life to the Lord at this meeting. The children and I returned to Nigeria in December 1991 to join him. The Lord had led him to start attending the New Covenant Church at this time and this has been our home church ever since. It's been wonderful growing under the leadership of brother Paul and sister Kate. They are not only our spiritual parents but have also been of tremendous blessings to us.

After having been in Architectural practice for about 12 years, the Holy Spirit led Femi to resign his partnership and we started another firm together in 1993. We ran this business for another 4 years before going into full time ministry. The entire family is now based in the UK where we now pastor our local branch of the New Covenant Church on Old Kent Road, Elephant and Castle, London. Going deeper for us meant giving up all to follow the leading of the Holy Spirit. This is why it is crucial to have a relationship with Him so that we can be sure that we are being led by Him. We believe we are in God's will for our lives and are ready to do whatever He requires of us.

In the year 2000, the Lord asked me a question. A question that will determine whether or not I was committed to serve Him all the days of my life. He said to me, 'Can you pay the price?' You see I felt that the transition between giving up our business and going into ministry would cause some financial strain in running the home. I believed I needed to help God by making more money to support my husband's salary. We had two teenagers and a toddler to feed and cloth, rent, bills and our general basic needs to meet.

God was indeed faithful in helping me set up a business, a hairdressing salon. I got a non-refundable grant from a group that assisted young businesses and also a two-year rent- free period on the premises. God allowed me for two years to discover whether I was going to trust Him to provide for us as a family or I was going to depend on my own strength. At the end of the first year, I began to lose my peace. The business had not broken even, but I knew God was also asking for my time. I spent most of the time in the salon counselling and praying for people. On several occasions, my clients come in and tell me I'm in the wrong business. "You ought to be in church", they often say to me. I went away for three days to seek God's face as all I wanted was to do His perfect will for my life. This was when He asked me the question 'Can you pay the price?' Was I willing to lose whatever prestige I thought I had at this time, was I willing to be criticised and referred to as a fanatic?

The Lord asked me a question that will determine whether or not I was committed to serve Him all the days of my life – 'Can you pay the price?'

The fact is, by the standard of the world, laying down our architectural practice and now the salon to serve the Lord does not seem to measure up. I understood the question, and my answer was 'Yes! Yes! Yes!' I had to answer yes. I came to realise the price is not greater than God's grace. I had misplaced my faith in the business instead of putting my faith in God. I packed up the business and joined my husband in ministry. I have not looked back since. I am not saying it is wrong to do business or that I'll never do business again, all I'm saying is that God wanted me at this time to give all my time to His service. I needed to go deeper, and to do that nothing else mattered to me.

Soon after I went into ministry, the Holy Spirit began to prompt me about doing more for the Lord. He said my light had to shine and quite honestly, I didn't know what else to do or how to even begin to go about it. The Holy Spirit went ahead and spoke to the National Overseer of the Church, Rev. Timothy Kolade that I should be released into ministry. God is so awesome. He has everything worked out even when we can't quite figure out how. God used Rev. Kolade to allow me to be the woman He has called me to be. Through the years, there have been those that have questioned the ministry of women, putting us in our place so to speak. There have been times I have been discouraged and felt like giving up, but Rev. Kolade always reminded me that God called me and can see me through. I believe all the gifts I received came from God. I never sought to go into ministry, but God is sovereign and the work is God's.

On the 8th of July 2001, I became an ordained minister of the New Covenant Church. Brother Paul laid hands on me and released me into my ministry. I don't believe I could have gone this far without the help of my friend, the Holy Spirit. I reverence you Holy Spirit.

<u>CAUGHT IN HIS GLORY</u>

In the same month of July 2001, Femi and I went to the Kenneth Hagin's Ministries Camp meeting in Tulsa Oklahoma. The Lord began to lead us to attend the meeting earlier on in the year. He had initially spoken to us concerning this trip in 1993. This time around, we knew we had to go as God wanted to do something specific in our lives. We attended the Camp meeting, which ran between the 21st to the 28th of July. Brother Hagin was a man of faith and had been miraculously healed of a deformed heart and incurable blood disease at the age of 17. He operated in the healing anointing, and his ministry has blessed many people.

We were taught faith in the morning, faith in the afternoon and faith in the evening. By the fourth day, faith had risen up in me that I could believe God for anything.

It was our first camp meeting, and we were amazed at the number of Christians under one roof praising and worshipping God together. It felt like heaven on earth and really gave us a little taste of what it will be like in heaven. We were taught faith in the morning, faith in the afternoon and faith in the evening. By the fourth day of the meeting, faith had risen up in me that I knew I could believe God for anything and get it. The bible says, "Faith cometh by hearing, and hearing by the word of God".

I began to ask the Lord to have His way in our lives. We knew God had allowed us to attend for a purpose. We had been obedient and travelled thousands of miles to be there. The meeting was to close on Saturday night and by Friday night, nothing had happened. I went to bed that night telling the Lord we had one more day, as if He didn't know, and that He should visit us at the meeting the next day.

Saturday morning, we must have been one of the first people to arrive at the Arena. We found seats on the third row, the first two rows were reserved, and we sat there soaking in every word we were taught. By the evening, which was to be the closing rally, we still managed to keep our seats on the third row.

This had to be it. Something had to happen now. We had a wonderful time of worship and at around 8:15 pm brother Hagin began to minister. He had been teaching on 'joy' and I had slightly begun to feel 'drunk' with laughter. I had wondered all week why people would just burst out laughing in the meetings. I thought they were a distraction and couldn't quite understand what was funny especially as the minister didn't seem to be saying anything funny. It was not that this experience was totally new to me though. I had found myself laughing hilariously during my quiet time with the Lord and had felt this was a personal thing between a man and his God. But to begin to laugh publicly and appear to be disrupting the service, this was new to me and up to this point, I thought was very wrong. I didn't know what it means when the bible talks about 'joy in the Holy Ghost'. Romans 14:17 says: 'For the kingdom of God is not a matter of eating and drinking, but of righteousness, peace and joy in the Holy Spirit'.

Ephesians 5:18 also says, 'Do not be drunk on wine, which leads to debauchery. Instead, be filled with the Spirit'. It's implied here that when you are filled with the Holy Spirit, it will feel like being drunk with wine. A drunken man is said to be 'under the influence of alcohol.' Another power takes over and he does things he would not normally do, though not necessarily pleasant things. In the same way, the Holy Spirit takes over when we are under His control and we are able to do things that we cannot do in our own strength. Sometimes you may just need to "jump in". You may not necessarily feel like laughing or dancing in the natural, but as you laugh or dance by faith, the Holy Spirit will do the rest.

This, I believe is the state I was, wanting to burst out in laughter, when I heard the Lord say to my spirit, 'tell your husband you love him'. Naturally, I wanted to say 'get thee behind me Satan'. This is a spiritual gathering and such thoughts should not be entering my heart at this time. But I knew it was the voice of the Holy Spirit and I obeyed the instruction right there in the meeting.

God had been dealing with me in the area of my love walk. I wanted to change my personality in order to "fit in", so I felt I had to work really hard to be who I was expected to be before I could be loved. A lot of factors were responsible for my feeling this way. I believed I could not have been loved since my parents had not planned to have me. I came along by 'accident'. I was quite small in frame as I grew up and always had to do extra to be noticed. On several occasions, people thought my younger siblings were older than me because of my stature. Coming into ministry and being a Pastors wife added to the challenges I faced. My husband was a perfectionist and wanted me to be perfect in every way. People were watching me, so I had to be careful how I talked, walked and dressed.

Jesus said in Matthew 22:39, "You shall love your neighbour as yourself". You cannot love others if you do not love and accept yourself as you are.

This is the state I was when we went to the camp meeting. I was very angry that I could not be "me". I was full of bitterness, resentment and was tired. Tired of having to live up to others expectations. I knew this issue was bothering me and needed to be dealt with. I had noticed they had counsellors and intercessors on ground, and I had gone to see one of them earlier on in the day. She assured me I was created in God's image and I was not to try and change my God-given personality, the way I look, my stature, background, the things I felt comfortable with, the things I like, all those things that makes me the individual He made me to be. God knew me before I was born. My frame was not hidden from Him when I was made in the secret place. He loves me the way I am.

She joined me in prayer, and I asked God to forgive me for not loving myself and for being so angry and bitter. I also forgave all those I thought were responsible for my being unhappy. It was not difficult for me to forgive at this point because I realised I had suffered enough hurt and pain and I just wanted to be free. God in His mercies healed my heart and I was able to receive His love for me. So when the Holy Spirit asked me to tell my husband I love him, He was helping me put a seal to the confessions I had made earlier on.

If you are struggling with loving yourself, then you may find it difficult to forgive, accept and love others. Find a Christian friend, counsellor or intercessor you can talk with and hand the situation over to God. He wants to heal your hurt and move you forward, but you must first learn to walk in love with all men. The bible says in 1 John 4:20, "If someone says 'I love God,' and hates his brother, he is a liar"

Love is an essential ingredient in our walk with God. We cannot say we love God without first loving our fellow Christians and we cannot have fellowship with God without having fellowship with our brothers and sisters in Christ.

When we become born again, the Holy Spirit comes to live in us with His potential for this tremendous life of love. He does not come apart from his holiness. The bible says the "love of God has been shed abroad in our hearts by the Holy Spirit". He is waiting on us to make us more loving, and there is nothing more important than learning to love. Every other spiritual force derives its action from love.

First Corinthians 13:4-8 clearly tells us how love behaves.

Love is an essential ingredient in our walk with God. We cannot say we love God without first loving our fellow Christians.

"Love endures long and is patient and kind; love never is envious nor boils over with jealousy, is not boastful or vainglorious, does not display itself haughtily. It is not conceited (arrogant and inflated with pride); it is not rude (unmannerly), and does not act unbecomingly. Love (God's love in us) does not insist on its own rights or its own way, for it not self - seeking; it is not touchy or fretful or resentful; it takes no account of the evil done to it. It does not rejoice at injustice and unrighteousness, but rejoices when right and truth prevail. Love bears up under anything and everything that comes, is ever ready to believe the best of every person, its hopes are fadeless under all circumstances, and it endures everything. Love never fails (never fades out or becomes obsolete or comes to an end)". (The Amplified Bible)

Love never fails. Nothing works without it and there can be no failure with it.

What God was about to do in my life depended on my walking in love with all men. To walk in the spirit is to walk in love. According to Galatians 5:22, Paul says:

"But the fruit of the Spirit is love, joy, peace, longsuffering, kindness, goodness, faithfulness, gentleness, self-control. Against such there is no law".

This means that when you are walking in the fruit of the spirit, there is no law that can bear witness against you because you are fulfilling all the requirements of the law. Therefore when you walk in love, no law can bear witness against you.

It is not the natural human love between husband and wife that God was asking for, even though this is just as important, he was drawing my attention to the fact that I could do nothing in His name outside of walking in love. This is what will bring me into victory in every area of my life. The Holy Spirit will prompt us anytime we fall out of love. He's our helper and convicts us whenever we miss it.

We need to search our hearts from time to time and judge ourselves against First Corinthians 13. If we find ourselves wanting in any area, we need to repent and fall back in line with our love walk.

Brother Hagin began to come down the steps and stood right in front of us. The two reserved rows were empty so we were more or less face to face with him. He paused and said in the past he used to call people out to lay hands on them for the impartation of gifts and the anointing of the Holy Spirit, but these days, (probably because of his age) the Lord had told him that as he walks around the meeting, people can 'catch' the anointing from where they are seated. I knew the Lord was speaking to me, that statement was for my benefit. I will have to 'catch' the anointing; the same way Elisha caught the mantle off Elijah.

> *I was caught up in what seemed to be a whirlwind. I felt so much power passing through me and if it didn't stop, I would explode.*

Almost immediately, Femi opened his bible to Hebrews 1:9 and showed it to me and I knew he wanted me to read it. This was the word the Lord had given us before we came to camp meeting. As soon as I read the words "You have loved righteousness and hated wickedness, therefore God, your God, has set you above your companions by anointing you with the oil of joy", I was caught up in what seemed to me to be whirlwind. I felt so much power, like high voltage electricity passing through me, and l thought if it didn't stop, I would explode. I cannot find words to explain what happened to me that evening, but God had certainly touched me. When I came back to myself so to speak, I realised I was on the floor and my shoes had been flung all over the place. I was helped back to my seat but I could not sit still. When I opened my mouth to speak, I could only speak in tongues. I was filled to overflowing by the Holy Spirit, and even after the service had ended, I could not walk out of the auditorium without assistance, my legs felt absolutely numb. Being 'slain' in the spirit as it's referred to, is quite scriptural. When Saul, later called Paul met the Lord Jesus on the road to Damascus in Acts 9:4, he fell slain to the ground. In John 18: 1-6, when the soldiers and Pharisees approached Jesus to arrest Him, they fell at His presence.

We must understand that when the natural comes in contact with the supernatural, the natural must bow. That is why, sometimes in worship, we cannot help but bow our knees to the Lord in total surrender. I am not saying you must be slain in the Spirit before you can receive anything from God. There have been other times when God has blessed me with a new gift in the place of prayer, without any obvious manifestations. The point I'm making here is that if you seek God with all of your heart and you are determined to fulfill His will for your life, he will show up.

Femi and some dear sisters managed to get me back to the hotel that night. I still could not communicate in English but carried on speaking in the Holy Ghost. God began to show me my assignment and referred me to scriptures in the bible to confirm His word to me. I fell asleep in this state. When I woke up the next day, I knew my life and ministry had changed and God had empowered me for service in the Kingdom. For me, the experience I had is not as important as the Word I got from the Lord. It gave me a sense of direction, purpose and calling.

God calls everyone uniquely by name and so you are not here by accident.

God calls everyone uniquely by name and so you are not here by accident. He is looking for hungry and searching hearts, men and women who want to reach the lost, doomed and dying souls all over the world. He has a purpose for you and I, and we must assume total responsibility for pursuing that call because we will be held accountable for our purpose in life.

I knew God had called me into ministry and was confirming the healing ministry He had previously spoken about. His gifts and call are irrevocable and He never withdraws them. Perhaps you feel God has changed His mind about His call upon your life and you are now looking to do other things, think again. He knew you before He called you. He knew your life, weaknesses, mistakes and sin and still had enough faith in you before He called you. He has not changed His mind about you. However, as I said before, you are accountable and will be responsible to carry out the call. Today, we run a healing school bimonthly in the Church with many testimonies of God's healing touch in the lives of the people. This, I know is just the beginning of greater things that God will yet do in this ministry. Whatever God has promised to do in your life, receive it by faith. He who has promised is faithful and He will do it.

The last six years have been wonderful. I have found fulfilment in what I am called to do. I now know the hope for which He has made me. God has allowed me to be in contact with so many beautiful people who have been of tremendous blessing to me. They have touched my life in one way or the other, encouraging me to get on with the work and giving me the opportunity to be myself.

If you are a new Christian and trying to find your feet in the Kingdom, God is calling you to a deeper fellowship with Him. There is much more to learn from the Holy Spirit. You need to get yourself into the presence of God. You may be wondering how. God promises that if we seek Him, we will find Him.

"And you will seek me and find me, when you search for Me with all your heart."

Jeremiah 29:13.

Ask the Holy Spirit to plant you in a living Church, somewhere you can fulfil God's call upon your life. Fellowship with other Christians by attending not only the Sunday service, but also the mid-week services. Get yourself some good Christian books, CD's and whatever else is available to help you grow spiritually.

As often as we can make it as a family, we attend the Kenneth Hagin's Ministries Camp Meeting, Kenneth Copeland's Believers Convention and Benny Hinn's Miracle Crusades. All these ministries and many others that we partner with have really blessed us and helped to keep us refreshed. For example, Gloria

Copeland's ministry to the sick has really encouraged me in my call to the Healing Ministry. I have always admired her boldness in teaching the Word of God, and heard her share how God had led her to start the healing school. It was her obedience to answer that 'call' and keep praying for the sick that challenged me to know that I can do it too. Your gender should not stop you from fulfilling your destiny. God will equip you and see you through.

PRAYING IN TONGUES

Prayer is one way that we can get closer to God and cultivate a deep and meaningful relationship with Him. He has called us into a loving relationship and seeks communication with us. Prayer is a dialogue and so as much as we speak to God, we must allow Him to speak back to us. Some of us have no difficulty speaking to God, but do you hear Him when He speaks back to you? Some of us on the other hand find it difficult knowing what to say and how to listen to him. When we have prayed in the language we understand we need now to pray in the language of heaven, in 'tongues', as the bible puts it.

"For he who speaks in a tongue does not speak to men but to God, for no one understands him; however, in the spirit he speaks mysteries."

1 Corinthians 14:2

This is where the Holy Spirit comes in to help us. Remember he is our helper, even in prayer. Romans 8:26 says:

"Likewise the Spirit also helps in our weaknesses. For we do not know what we should pray for as we ought, but the Spirit Himself makes intercession for us with groanings which cannot be uttered."

Prayer is a dialogue. As much as we speak to God, we must allow Him to speak back to us.

You need to ask the Holy Spirit to help you pray, and not only to pray, but also to have an understanding of that which you have prayed about.

What do we mean by speaking or praying in tongues? Speaking in tongues have nothing to do with the mind or the ability to learn a language you are not familiar with. It is basically speaking supernaturally by the Holy Spirit a language never learned nor understood by you, the speaker. It is an utterance given by the Holy Spirit and it usually manifests when people are baptized in the Holy Spirit. It is an evidence of the fact that the Holy Spirit has come to dwell in fullness in the heart of the believer. Jesus said to his disciples in Mark 16:17:

"And these signs will follow those who believe: In my name they will cast out demons; they will speak with new tongues;"

Speaking in tongues is one of the supernatural signs Jesus said will follow those who believe in Him. However, the area I want us to focus on is speaking in tongues as a devotional gift. It is to be used to assist us in our prayer life, in worshipping and praising God.

It is good to pray in tongues for a while. Ephesians 6:18 encourage us to pray in the spirit at all times. We have been taught in the Full Gospel Businessmen's Fellowship to speak in tongues for at least one hour a day. When I first started practising this, I shut my eyes and thought I must have prayed for nothing less than an hour. When I checked my watch, I had only been praying for fifteen minutes. Initially, it was tough getting used to, but after a while, it became part of my special time with the Lord and I started feeling I wasn't getting enough. God has much He wants to share with us. When we pray in tongues, we should pray as I said earlier for understanding of that which we have prayed about. On some occasions, I have found that after spending time praying in tongues, I have had an understanding of what I had been praying about. Seeking understanding however should not be our main focus. Our focus should be on the fact that we know we are praying according to God's will for our lives.

Just before I got pregnant with our last son, I had been praying in tongues and I later had an understanding that God was instructing me to begin to get ready for a move. I knew He was asking me to start packing suitcases and get our property in order, ready for a move abroad. We had no specific plans to relocate at this time, and it didn't really seem to make a lot of sense. However, I began to sort out our properties, literarily packed up my whole kitchen, wrapping up plates and cups and all the breakables. I gave away most of the children's clothes they no longer needed and just waited for the next direction. Soon after that, I discovered I was pregnant and had begun to feel very ill. God had revealed to Femi in a dream after a powerful church meeting we had in 1996 with our General Overseer, brother Paul, that the key to our blessings had been tied ever since we decided to stop having children. It wasn't that we didn't want anymore, it was the trauma I went through with the pregnancies of our first two children that brought us to this decision. We prayed about this revelation, repented and basically told God we were fine with the two he had blessed us with. However, we knew we wanted to be in His perfect will for our lives. God had better plans for us and so He started preparing us for them. We may not understand why we need to go through certain things in life, but we must trust God that He knows best.

One would have thought God would make this pregnancy go smoothly, especially as it came on account of God's revelation. It turned out to be the most traumatic of all. The nine months of pregnancy were the longest nine months of my life. I was miserable and angry with everyone around me, including God. Why did He allow me to go through so much pain? As I couldn't keep food down, I lost a lot of weight and must have spent seven out of the nine months in bed. The most irritating part is that I had no desire to talk. It was actually painful making conversation with anybody. I didn't want to read or write, I just wanted to be left alone. I believe God shut my mouth to stop me from saying the wrong things. I spent a lot of the time meditating on the Word of God that I already knew. It was only that which I had stored up in my spirit that I was able to meditate on. But guess who was there encouraging me all the way? My friend, the Holy Spirit. Nobody can understand what I went through, what was going on in my mind, but He was there, He saw me through, He gave me grace. I could not have gone through the nine months without His help. Sometimes we are angry with ourselves and with God for situations we cannot change or do anything about. The challenges I faced during the time of pregnancy didn't go away, but God gave me grace by His Spirit to help me through. His grace will always be sufficient for you.

At 3 am on the 4th of April 1997, I woke up from sleep and heard what must be a mass choir singing 'Alleluia! Alleluia! Alleluia! The strife is o'er, the battle done…' I knew this song as we used to sing it at Easter in the Anglican Church. As soon as the choir stopped singing, I went into labour and I knew it was all over. Heaven was already rejoicing with me. That day, John (God's gracious gift) was born weighing 4060 kg. How he got to be that big is a miracle in itself.

Don't wait until you are in some kind of trouble or in need of help before you begin to pray. You never know what the Holy Spirit will have you pray about, but I believe I had already prayed through this pregnancy even before it came to be. That is the beauty of praying in tongues. You may not understand what you are saying, but the Holy Spirit makes intercession for you. It was in the place of prayer that I had been led to start packing. He was getting me ready for what was ahead of me. He knew I would not have the strength to pack in pregnancy, and also knew we would be relocating to the United Kingdom. My obedience to His instruction that came in the place of prayer helped me tremendously when we finally had to move.

A lot of people say they cannot find the time to pray in tongues. Try and make time. There are a lot of activities that we get involved in that are not profitable to us. Plan your day, even if it means getting up a little bit earlier than you currently do. One of the things the Holy Spirit also taught me when I was nursing my baby and could not really keep to a scheduled plan or time of prayer is that I can pray 'as I go'. Remember He lives in you and He's with you all the time, so you can pray in tongues while you shower, garden, cook, clean the house or whatever else you find yourself doing. I often pray in tongues when I'm driving and alone in the car. If the journey takes an hour, I would have prayed for an hour by the time I reach my destination. I strongly advise praying in tongues as often as you can. It helps you mature spiritually as Jude verse 20 says:

"But you, beloved, building yourselves up on your most holy faith, praying in the Holy Spirit."

When the Holy Spirit filled me with His Power as I said in the last chapter, I immediately began to speak in tongues and must have carried on for hours until I fell asleep. The Holy Spirit was interceding for me according to God's will for my life. We all need the Holy Spirit's help when it comes to prayers so that we are sure we are not only praying God's perfect will for us, but also that our lives are being enriched spiritually.

We cannot talk about the baptism in the Holy Ghost without mentioning the gifts of the spirit or Spiritual gifts. Paul lists these gifts in 1 Corinthians 12:8-11:

"For to one is given the word of wisdom through the Spirit, to another the word of knowledge through the same Spirit, to another faith by the same Spirit, to another gift of healings by the same Spirit, to another the working of miracles, to another prophecy, to another different kinds of tongues, to another the interpretation of tongues. But one and the same Spirit works all these things, distributing to each one Individually as He wills."

The baptism of the Holy Ghost opens the door for us to operate in these supernatural gifts of the Spirit. They are available for everyone. 1 Corinthians 14:1 says we are to desire spiritual gifts. As a believer, a born again child of God, we should do the works that Jesus did, and signs and wonders should follow when we preach the Word.

If you read the book of the Acts of the Apostles, you will see the operation of the gifts of the Spirit in the lives of the apostles in the early Church. It was the gifts of the Spirit that enabled Peter raise the crippled man at the beautiful gate in Acts 3 and to raise Dorcas from the dead in Acts 9. It was the gifts of the Spirit that empowered the apostles to perform signs and wonders among the people, causing Philip and Stephen to do the miraculous. The operation of the gifts of the Spirit in every case brought many to be added unto the Church as they believed in the Lord Jesus Christ.

Be encouraged to stir up the gift of God which is in you (2 Timothy 1:6) so that you can effectively go into the world and make disciples of all nations as Jesus instructs us to do in Matthew 28:19.

WORSHIP IN THE SPIRIT

Praying in tongues and operating the gifts of the Spirit are wonderful, but it is also important that you are a worshipper. Jesus said to the Samaritan woman in John 4:23-24:

> "But the hour is coming and now is, when
> the true worshippers will worship the Father
> in spirit and truth; for the Father is seeking
> such to worship him. God is Spirit, and those

who worship Him must worship in spirit and truth."

Worship is the way into God's presence. God told Moses in the Old Testament how to come into His presence. He gave him a plan and a pattern to build which is called the Tabernacle. The Tabernacle of Moses had three parts, The Outer Court, the Holy Place and the Holy of Holies. As a person, you also have three parts as discussed earlier on: spirit, soul and body. With your body you are world-conscious, with your soul, you are self-conscious and with your spirit, you are God-conscious. These three parts can be directly related to the Tabernacle, your body being the Outer Court, your soul, the Holy Place and your spirit, the Holy of Holies. The Holy of Holies is where we want to be. It's the very presence of God. In Hebrews 10:19, the bible says

"Therefore, brethren having boldness to enter the Holiest by the blood of Jesus."

The Holy Spirit is saying here that we are expected to enter into the Holy of Holies.

With your body, you are world-conscious, with your soul, you are self-conscious and with your spirit, you are God-conscious.

Start off with some songs of praise, psalms, and possibly a poem from your heart. Talk to Him in prayer, even with your silence. Bow your heart to Him in reverence and worship. Your head or mind will struggle with you in keeping still and concentrating only on Him, but be persistent. The bible says in Psalms 100:4:

"Enter into His gates with thanksgiving and into His courts with praise."

Learn how to move from the Outer court to the Holy place and then the Holy of Holies. You begin by thanking God in the outer court (body), this leads to praising Him in the Holy place (soul), and you worship in the Holy of Holies (spirit). God desires our worship and in the Holy of Holies, that's what you do. You are now in the presence of God. Oh what a glorious place to be. The experience cannot be put to words. It's indescribable. It is the presence of God that creates worship. Most times if I'm not already on my face in worship, the presence of God in the room causes me to 'fall' or bow my knees before Him. God does tremendous things when we are in His presence. Whatever you need, you'll find in His presence. When I've needed a 'dose of joy' as I like to put it, I've asked the Holy Spirit to fill me with His joy, knowing that the bible says in Psalms 16: 11...

"In Your presence is fullness of joy, at Your right hand are pleasures forevermore."

Joy unspeakable well up within me and I begin to laugh in the Holy Ghost. As I said previously, you can be filled with so much joy that you feel like a drunkard and cannot stop laughing.

You can be filled with so much joy that you feel like a drunkard and can't stop laughing.

Have you ever been intimate with the Holy Spirit? Can you move the heart of Jesus with your worship and love for Him? Can you truly say you have been in His presence? If you cannot answer yes to any of these questions, then begin to covet a closer walk with the Holy Spirit. Fall in love with the Holy Spirit and you are in love with Jesus. Access into God's presence comes from your relationship with His Spirit.

I believe this is that time when the knowledge of the glory of God will cover the earth as the waters cover the sea. This is the time that as we worship, healings will come, deliverances will come, the Power of God is available and we come into blessings. Men will be set free, the unbelievers will believe and run to the altar for forgiveness of their sins. Why? Because the Glory of God has filled the temple, and everything else must bow.

__MY BEST FRIEND__

The Holy Spirit has been to me all Jesus said He is in His word. He bears many names: He's been my Counsellor and Comforter, the Spirit of Truth, the Spirit of Life, the Spirit of Grace, the Spirit of Glory, the Spirit of revelation, the Eternal Spirit, my intercessor, my guide, my teacher and much more than I can ever record. But most of all, He has been my friend, and so I simply call Him "My Best friend". Think about it, what do best friends do? If you have a good relationship with your friend, you will spend time together, you might talk for hours on the phone. You'll share old and new experiences, encouraging and advising one another. You go shopping together, may have lunch, dinner or even go on holidays together. You trust each other, and you are ready to go out of your way to please your friend. You laugh and cry together. You are buddies and love one another. This is whom the Holy Spirit is, dependable, never failing. I remember the times He has gently corrected me in love, asked me to check the oven, front door or anything I had carelessly left unattended, He's helped me locate things I had misplaced, told me what to say or do in tricky situations, helped me from getting stuck in traffic jams, constantly encouraged me when down. He's done so much too numerous to mention.

> **He is not a force or a thing.
> He is a person, He is God.**

He continues to work in me as I give Him room to do so. He strengthens me, guides me into all truth, reveals the deep things of God to me and imparts me with the Power of God. He does not speak of Himself, but glorifies Jesus.

He is not a force or a thing. He is a Person. He is God. We are meant to fellowship with Him and perhaps up till now, you didn't know you could grieve Him by ignoring Him, refusing to recognise His presence or even be obedient to His instructions. If you decide not to call your best friend anymore, it will lead to you not spending time together anymore and obviously, he or she will be grieved. It will appear as if you have found a new friend and you don't need their friendship anymore. Rev.2: 4 says the Church at Ephesus has forsaken her first love and asks that they repent and do the things they did at first. Have you forsaken your first love? Perhaps you had a wonderful relationship with the Holy Spirit in the past, but the cares of this world have shifted your gaze and you have wandered off. Why don't you put things right, do as suggested in Revelations chapter 2, repent and ask the Lord to forgive you. Ask the Holy Spirit to fill you afresh; he's waiting on you to ask. He's a gentleman and won't force Himself on you. Go ahead and take that bold step of faith.

You may be a churchgoer, but it will take more than church membership and water baptism for you to make heaven.

If you have never surrendered your life to the Lord Jesus Christ, but have read this book this far, congratulations! You may be a churchgoer, but it will take more than church membership and being baptized in water for you to make heaven. Jesus said, "....You must be born again" (John 3:7). This simply means you accept Jesus into your heart as your Lord and Saviour. A simple prayer will lead you to your destiny and you too can begin to enjoy the benefits of salvation. You too can become a friend of the Holy Spirit. Pray the following prayer in faith, and Jesus will be your Lord.

Heavenly Father, I come to you in the name of Jesus. Your Word says, "Whoever shall call on the name of the Lord shall be saved" and "If you confess with your mouth the Lord Jesus, and believe in your heart that God raised him from the dead, you will be saved" (Acts2:21, Romans10:9). I believe my salvation will be the result of your Holy Spirit giving me new birth by coming to live in me. I also believe that if I ask, you will fill me with your Spirit and give me the ability to speak in other tongues. I believe your Word and I confess that Jesus is Lord. I believe in my heart that you raised Him up from the dead. Thank you for coming into my heart, for giving me your Holy Spirit and for being Lord over my life. Amen.

Heaven rejoices with you now as you have just received the greatest miracle of salvation. You have made the most important decision you will ever make in life and you cannot possibly remain the same. Ask the Holy Spirit to begin to teach you how to walk with God and begin to enjoy the purpose for which God has called you.

Fellowship with the Holy Spirit on a daily basis. Learn to hear his voice and make Him your Counsellor, Helper, Teacher and Friend. Thirst for Him, yearn for Him, love Him and reverence Him. Do whatever you need to do, but most of all, make sure you know Him.

I thank my Heavenly Father for my salvation, for my redemption, and for giving me the Holy Spirit.

"In Him you also trusted, after you heard the word of truth, the gospel of your salvation; in whom also, having believed, you were sealed with the Holy Spirit of promise, who the guarantee of our inheritance until the redemption of the purchased possession, to the praise of his glory." Ephesians 1:13-14.

There is much to do in the Kingdom of God. Find your place and begin to fulfil the purpose for which He has called you.

"The grace of our Lord Jesus Christ, and the love of God, and the communion of the Holy Spirit be with you all. Amen."

(2 Corinthians 13:14)

If you have prayed the prayer at the end of this book, congratulations and welcome into the family of God. If you will like to enquire further or if we can be of any help to you, please contact us at:

themasters_touch@hotmail.com or telephone +44 (0) 20 7473 2866

AUTHOR BIOGRAPHY

Atinuke Omisade is a qualified Architect but is now in full time ministry. She is an ordained minister of the New Covenant Church, a teacher of the Word and operates in the healing ministry. Having been delivered from the 'spirit of infirmity', she has compassion for the sick and co-ordinates the healing school and healing rooms in her church, and has seen many healed and delivered from various sicknesses and diseases.

She is the minister-in charge of the Women's Ministry and shares her insights into women issues.

She understands the value of intimacy with God and has taught extensively about the Holy Spirit and His work.

Atinuke also co-ordinates "FOODAID", a project set up to feed the hungry in less privileged countries.

She and her husband Femi live in London United Kingdom. They pastor a branch of the New Covenant Church. They have three children Antoinette, Anthony and John.

CPSIA information can be obtained at www.ICGtesting.com
Printed in the USA
BVOW07s1511110714

358920BV00001B/13/P